love
POEMS
we love

EDWARD H. ESSEX

ISBN: 978-0-9910364-6-2

Publisher: Words In The Works LLC   info@wordsintheworks.com

Also by Edward H. Essex: Remains To Be Seen–*An Erotic Thriller*
Available for Kindle and in paperback at Amazon.com

contents

In this book you will find occasional blank pages.
Edward invites you to jot down your passing thoughts,
feelings, or maybe even a poem or two of your own.

As he does in *Remains To Be Seen*, Edward writes
in both the male and female voice.

with thanks

to Kathleen, Marylou, Jane, and other dear friends and
readers for insisting I get these poems into print.

Your eyes, your eyes, they paralyze.
Yes, this is for you.

don't
STOP
there

Don't Stop There

I lick
Your foot.
And then
Your calf.
My tongue
Is on
A sensuous
Path.

I rest
My tongue
Behind
Your knee.
Then up
Your thigh.
Now…
What's this
I see?

May need further research
to complete this poem.

kissing
YOU

Kissing You

The first time
We just brushed lips,
A kiss that
Touched the air.
But it
Was enough
To wonder...
What else
There might
Be there?

We met again,
And kissed again,
This time,
Soft and long.
I kissed
Your face,
Your neck,
Your breasts.
The kiss went
On and on.

I had thought
About your lips.
That first kiss
Was so fleeting.
And then
You told me,
You had too.
A second kiss
You were...
A-waiting.

a flash of NEED

A Flash of Need

Irresistible urge,
A flash of need,
A want of love,
That won't recede.

This luscious lust,
I will allow,
Not tomorrow,
But now, right now.

My blouse unbuttoned,
Naked he lies,
I remove my skirt,
I feast my eyes.

I want him now,
Desire he feeds.
I must relieve,
This flash of need.

naked THOUGHTS

Naked Thoughts

They lay naked
Nothing to hide.
Plotting, wondering,
Side by side.

Will they be married
Surrounded by friends?
Lasting happiness,
Joy without end?

Who will come?
He wonders aloud.
—Why, everyone we know,
It'll be quite a crowd.

What if somebody wanders
Right in off the street?
—Well, they'd watch us get married,
And then stay to eat.

Sooner or later,
Will that day come?
When the wondering ends,
And they live as one?

HANDS
that see

Hands That See

My hands
Search the dark,
Like a flashlight
In the night.
Feeling your body,
My fingers
Are my sight.
My hands are candles,
Burning bright.
And when they touch
Your softest skin,
My hands my mind
Excites.

what was i THINKING?

What Was I Thinking?

Feeling complete,
I thought my life whole.
You have eased in
And captured my soul.
Need? Not I.
But desire? Oh Yes!
Unaware until now,
I would never have guessed.

Alone, not allowing
Alone to deplete me.
Together I find,
Together completes me.

Built my own walls
And closed every shade.
Content with all
Decisions I made.
Not knowing just how
An open heart could
Feel with another—
Yet you understood.

I said I was whole,
No one would deplete me.
Allowed no space
For love to complete me.
Did not know love,
But know it now.
Opened my heart.
With you, somehow.

cont. over

Separate existence,
We lived life apart.
Now we're together,
Sharing one heart.
You now complete me.
Though I am still whole
What was I thinking?
You've captured my soul.

Alone, not allowing
Alone to deplete me.
Together I find,
Together completes me.

what are YOU *thinking?*

sleepy LOVE

Sleepy Love

Neither asleep, nor awake,
I seem to be.
Yet in waking dreams,
You come to me.
The softest touch,
My body feels.
Your fingertips,
Like silky wheels.
No sound, no talk,
Just silent dark.
Towards you now,
My body arcs.
Then your body,
Complete and whole,
Fills my being,
Mind and soul.
We reach together,
Heaven sent.
Arrive together,
And then, we're spent.
As pillow bound,
I am once more,
Asleep? Awake?
I'm still not sure.

lady on a SWING

Lady on a Swing

I have this
Mind's image
Of her
On a swing.
A picture of
Happiness.
Her heart
Seems to sing.

I imagine
Her flying
Toward me—
And now,
She lets go
Of the swing,
And I catch her
Somehow.

We stumble
A little,
But upright
We stay.
My hands round
Her waist.
Then together
We sway.

She smoothes
Her black dress.
And removes her

cont. over

Dark shades.
Her brown eyes
Are dancing,
In the light
Of the glade.

I imagine
The moment
Our lips
Softly meet.
I can taste her
Already,
So tender
And sweet.

Will we–
Swing together?
Who knows?
As they say.
But it's fun,
As of now.
And long may
That stay.

what are
YOU
thinking?

she needs a
HUG

She Needs a Hug

Done at last,
She beats a path,
To my front door.

Her day was hell,
She shouts and yells.
A virtual war.

A quiet cry,
She wipes her eyes,
Her wine I pour.

Before we eat,
Our bodies meet,
And spirits soar.

Food at last,
Warm looks are cast,
Our day explored.

And then goodbye,
A kiss; a sigh,
Tomorrow, more.

good WOMAN

Good Woman

You are a good woman,
Sent down from heaven,
Although you are human,
The perfect someone.

I am your true man,
I will be your good man,
I feel like a new man.
This, is an omen.

You are a good woman,
I recline on a cushion,
You rub me with lotion,
And elsewhere, can't mention.

You are a good woman,
I'm filled by your passion,
I adore your attention,
You are love on a mission.

NEXT
to me

Next to Me

Sitting here
On these
Glorious isles,
I am
Four thousand,
Nine hundred,
Miles
From your smiles.
But you're
Next to me,
On the beach
Where I'm at.
Never
A moment—
Did I
Ever doubt that.
All along you've
Been here,
With your
Sapphire eyes.
It's as if
We had
Never—
Said our
Goodbyes.

paralyzing EYES

Paralyzing Eyes

From across the room,
Or across the street.
If you're next to me,
Or the opposite seat.
The first thing I see,
Are your incredible eyes.
I'm stopped in my tracks.
I am paralyzed.
They hold me firm,
The stare me down.
They grip me tight,
They dance around.
You are they
And they are you.
The most incredible shade
Of the most incredible blue.
When your beautiful eyes
Are cast on me,
I see all the skies
And the deepest of seas.
Your eyes, your eyes,
Your beautiful eyes.
I'm stopped in my tracks.
I am paralyzed.

dearest MISS *lovely*

Dearest Miss Lovely

I look up from my cellphone
And there you are.
Striding long legs towards me,
Away from your car.

The restaurant's closed, I said.
Oh no, you cried.
I liked you already
But my feelings, I hide.

We went to another place
Just down the street.
Not particularly romantic
For the first time we meet.

But you told me of you;
And I told you of me.
And the thought crossed my mind
That you and I—could become We.

I call you Miss Lovely;
And you do look the part.
Exquisitely regal.
I'm losing my heart.

Those incredible cheekbones
And flaxen blond hair.
Those piercing blue eyes;
I melt at your stare.

cont. over

When you turn toward me;
You neck held with grace.
Then beauty composes
All over your face.

But dearest Miss Lovely,
It's not beauty alone.
For without and within–
You're in a class of your own.

what are YOU *thinking?*

all he
COULD
think of

All He Could Think Of

He woke this morning
To a glorious sunrise.
But all he could think of
Was the light in your eyes.

The sky was golden
Tinged by red hue.
But all he could think of
Was your brilliant blue.

He woke this morning
Like mornings just past.
And all he could think of
Was you first and last.

heavenly HALF *hour*

Heavenly Half-Hour

Thirty minutes,
One half-hour.
Eighteen hundred seconds,
We devour.

Stolen moments
Are what we have.
In between this,
We grab some of that.

No coffee or sandwiches,
On our lunch break.
It's off with our clothes
And make no mistake.

Sometimes it's only
A telephone call,
But total nudity
Is our Golden Rule.

Of one thing we're certain,
This love we have found.
Squeezed into 30 minutes
Is a love without bounds.

TULIPS
from my lover

Tulips From My Lover

My lover bought me tulips,
Upright in a bunch.
Gold and red and yellow,
I love them oh so much.
They've become a little tired,
But still lovely in the way…
They rest their heads
On the tabletop,
For me to love…another day.

nose to the ROSE

Nose to the Rose

I followed my nose
Because my nose knows.
And what this nose knows,
Is the sweet scent of you.

I followed my nose,
And what do you suppose?
Where did it go?
But to a love that is true.

I followed my nose
Led by my toes,
To you, my dear rose,
I love you, I do.

she GLANCED *at me*

She Glanced at Me

She glanced at me,
I glimpsed the future—
But I didn't know it then.

She glanced at me,
The briefest look.
And then she glanced again.

She glanced at me,
Just one more time.
It seemed to linger on.

She glanced at me—
I glanced back.
And then her eyes were gone.

waking THOUGHTS

Waking Thoughts

I wake,
I'm hard-
Pressed
To sleep.
I dreamt
I was…
Inside you
Deep.
My mind
Caressed
The thought
Of you.
I wonder
If…
Thoughts
Wake
You too?

ALONE
i am not

Alone

Fuzzy and warm
Alone in my spot.
As I lay with my thoughts
Alone I am not.

Reading your words
Your image I find.
I am lying alone
With you on my mind.

Music and thoughts, you
Weave through my soul.
Alone I am not
With you I feel whole.

Fuzzy and warm
Alone in my spot.
With you on my mind
Alone I am not.

ecstasy of
CONNECTION

Ecstasy of Connection

The phone rings
And I know it's you.
You think a thought
And I do too.
Each waking moment
You're on my mind.
This is a love
Of a different kind.
Emotional bonds
And mutual liking.
Sharing trust
And tears and crying.
We once crossed paths
And crossed again.
But this time round
We said Amen.
A lifetime searching
For the missing part.
The puzzle piece
That completes our heart.
They talk of chemistry,
But we have more,
An Ecstasy of Connection,
A Heavenly Rapport.

TOGETHER *at last*

Together at Last

Separate lives
In the same little town.
When you were up,
I might have been down.

Parallel paths
No encounter we had.
When I was happy,
You might have been sad.

Living apart
So near yet so far.
Did we look up
And gaze the same star?

Then under one roof
The look that said–Yes!
We fell madly in love,
Nothing more, nothing less.

Our eyes, then our hearts,
Our bodies we tethered.
Together at last,
And at last, we're together.

ISABELLA

Isabella

There's a fella,
Who saw
Isabella.
Liked what he saw,
And decided
To tell her.

There's a fella,
Who met
Isabella.
Thought she was nice,
If fact,
Rather stellar.

There's a fella,
Who likes
Isabella.
She's that bright star,
They call
The Capella.

There's a fella,
He's with
Isabella,
On some sandy beach,
Un—der
An um—brella.

cont. over

There's a fella,
And his girl,
Isabella.
Maybe they'll star
In the next
Great novella.

what are
YOU
thinking?

she WEARS it well

She Wears It Well

Cowboy boots,
Sequined skirt,
Funky coat,
Stylish shirt,
White silk blouse,
Well cut jeans,
Elegant tops,
Those kind of things.
Lovely lady,
Maiden fair,
But it's not
Just her,
It's the clothes
She wears.

hazy THOUGHTS

Hazy Thoughts

You lower your chin,
And then you begin–
To drive me crazy.

You raise your eyes,
In slight surprise–
Fresh as a daisy.

You flick your hair,
Give me that stare–
Sexy. And racey.

And then you smile,
I am beguiled.
My thoughts go hazy.

FOOTSTEPS

Footsteps

You've left my side,
But not for long.
Your distant footsteps,
Create a song.

I lie awake with
Thoughts of you—
I wonder if
You sense me too.

I will not stir;
I'll lie alone.
Until you sense
I need you home.

You've left my side
But not for long.
Approaching footsteps
Complete our song.

i LIKE you

I Like You

Your eyes are brown,
They stare me down,
I like you.

Your body tall,
Good looks and all,
I like you.

That lovely smile,
Wide as a mile,
I like you.

Cascading mane,
Your lively brain,
I like you.

The soul you bare,
Your gentle air,
I really, really…like you.

wanna MAKE *out?*

Wanna Make Out?

First Light,
Post Fight,
Shared Shower,
Found Hour.
Romantic Walk,
Tender Talk,
Wanna make out?
Dance Floor,
Empty Store,
Parked Car,
Dark Bar.
Irish Whiskey,
Feeling Frisky,
Wanna make out?
Date Night,
Moon Bright,
Fore-Play,
Long Day,
Hours Passed,
Fading Fast,
Wanna make out?

good MORNING

Good Morning

You faced away
And as you lay,
Your shoulders
Gently shrugged.

I turned to you,
Desire grew,
My arms around
You, hugged.

I kissed your neck,
Caressed your ear.
With words cooed,
Like a dove.

You turned around–
My body found,
And wrapped me
In your love.

A gentle kiss,
Then welded bliss,
And fire
Without warning.

Body scent and
Passions spent.
And then you said,
"Good morning."

life WITHOUT *sex?*

Life Without Sex?

You might think I'm old, 'cos there's gray in my hair.
And secretly wonder...if gray is down there.

You cannot imagine what I do with my bloke.
At my age sex is some kind of joke!

But age as I see it is not a just a number.
And if you don't have a bloke, try a cucumber.

Life without sex? I've tried it, it's bland!
At least there are dildos and using one's hand!

Lotions and potions, leather and lace,
My eye has a twinkle...there's a smile on my face.

Bumps in the night...then muffled screams.
Nightmares or sex? Lovemaking or dreams?

Fifty something? Sixty something? Who gives a care?
If the body parts work and desire is there.

So wear earplugs if you don't like the sound
Of bumps in the night when we're fooling around.

The sex is amusing and so is the notion
Of questions and whispers, what's all the commotion?

"Are they getting it on?" In this you can trust—
We're consenting adults, driven by lust!

cont. over

Fireworks and sonnets, it's different each time.
Conversation and gymnastics all intertwined.

All kidding aside, the sex is real nice.
Three to four times a week(day) seems to suffice.

what are YOU *thinking?*

our
SKY

Our Sky

You whisper "Look up."
I tilt my head.
We see the sunrise
From our bed.

Vibrant colors.
Colors bright.
Our morning filled
With morning light.

Day Two

You call "Come out."
I come to you.
We look to heaven
It's nothing but blue.

Vibrant sapphire.
Blue so bright.
Our midday filled
With pure delight.

Day Three

Skyward I glance.
You, on my mind.
I find a grey sky
Of the stormiest kind.

cont. over

Turbulent grey.
The grey of sorrow.
Though the sun is hidden
There's hope for tomorrow.

Day Four

We look out together
At new fallen snow.
Behind linear clouds
A shy sun does glow.

Orange streaks.
Yellow lines bold.
Highlight the clouds
Ignoring the cold.

what are
YOU
thinking?

you
STAYED

You Stayed

You stayed
One night,
Then two,
Then three.
This weekend,
You and I
Were we.
It was
Of course,
A fitting move.
'Cos once again,
Our love
We proved.
From Friday's night
To Monday's day.
Fun and laughter,
All the way.
We wake
Once more,
But this time
Slow,
Let's hold on tight
Before you go.

in between...the SHEETS

In Between

In between
These dreams
I stroke—
Your neck,
Your back,
Your legs.
Thoughts
Of you,
I want you,
I do…
In between…

The Sheets

White,
Washed,
Clean and
Fresh.
Now tangled,
Crumpled,
By our
Flesh.

lingering YOU

Lingering You

From room to room
I find you.
Your perfume lingers on.
You're fragrant here
Beside me.
Even when you're gone.

COME?

Come?

An ambiguous question:
Will you come with me?
It could mean in his bed
Or across the blue sea.

I'm fine with both
So my answer is "Yes!"
Nighty or flip-flops?
I'll just have to guess.

unscheduled
LOVE

Unscheduled Love

In the sun,
In the rain,
In the bed
With a view.
On the cliffs,
On the beach,
Just me
With you.

On the rocks,
In the sand,
We climb,
We walk.
Making memories,
Sharing moments,
We listen,
We talk.

We dance,
We laugh,
We eat
Holding hands.
Do headstands,
Walk labyrinths,
Find treasures
In the sand.

Light touches,
Soft whispers,
Along skin
Fingers trace.

cont. over

Back rubs,
Spine kisses,
Minds wander,
Hearts race.

No alarm clocks,
No agenda,
Spontaneous
And fun.
Love with
No schedule,
Under stars
And the sun.

what are
YOU
thinking?

full
MOON
full heart

Full Moon-Full Heart

I woke up
To a full moon
This morning.
He had forgotten
To go back to bed.
I woke up
To a full moon
This morning.
Thoughts of you,
Going round in my head.
I woke up
To a full moon
This morning.
Shining down
From a golden, red sky.
I woke up
To a full moon
This morning.
And then I started to cry.
I don't think I
Shed tears of sadness.
No, this was more like
A needed release.
I stayed close to
God and to you, love.
And there I found
A sweet peace.

cont. over

I woke up
To a full moon
This morning.
My day, I was
Ready to start.
I woke up
To a full moon
This morning.
Full moon, Full life,
Full heart.

what are
YOU
thinking?

a FEAST *of you*

A Feast of You

My appetizer
And main course.
My salad
And dessert.
My soup,
My snack,
No food I lack,
Not even
Blue Roquefort.
The main menu,
And tasty stew,
Your perfume
Sweet as dill.
Such nourishment
You are to me—
I'm careful
Not to spill.
I eat you up
With relish.
I can never
Get enough.
Your body is
The perfect dish.
My Fav-or-ite
Food stuff.

APPLE *pie*

Apple Pie

Make,
Bake,
From oven,
Take.

Cool,
Drool,
Fetch spatula
Tool.

Sliced,
Spice,
The nose
Enticed.

Sigh,
Cry,
For your
Apple Pie.

You,
Cream,
Delicious
Dream.

Have you ever eaten apple pie
with cream in bed? You really should.

love you
BUT NOT
tofu

Love You But Not Tofu

Give me chicken,
Give me stew,
Give me lamb shanks,
But not Tofu.
Give me Stilton,
A real fondue.
A sweet, ripe pear;
Forget Tofu.

Give me grapes,
Berries blue.
Peas and carrots,
I hate Tofu.
Give me bread,
And steak to chew.
Give me real food;
And I'll love you.

one EYE. on the pie

One Eye on the Pie

With a sigh,
She says goodbye.
She looks me in the eye.
"Soon I'll be by,
To rub your thigh–
And eat your...
Shepherd's pie."

still
HERE

Still Here

I open my eyes
And think of you.
Every morning
I always do.

At first last night,
We were together.
I wanted you
More than ever.

But then there came
An urgent need—
And from my side
You had to leave.

I wanted to
Hold on to you
But leaving was
The right thing to do.

And though you left
You were still here.
In my heart and thoughts
So clear.

L*at*AST

At Last

At last, when all these dreary hours
Have gone and when this day is past
The time can once again be ours,
I'll hold you close—at last, at last!
I've missed your touch, my dear soul mate
The sweetest thoughts I did allow
Pictures of love that came so late,
My soul shall keep them always now!

~With apologies to Elizabeth Akers Allen.

WHISPERING
in your ear

Whisper

Sweet and low,
Nice and slow.
I whisper
In your ear.
Saying all
The naughty things,
I know you
Love to hear.
It seems to work
Most every time.
My voice a
Gentle hum.
On our
Erotic journey,
We don't go...
But always come.

REMAINS
to be seen

Remains To Be Seen

Do you
Or don't you?
Will you
Or won't you?
Can we
Or can't we?
Shall we
Or shan't we?
Are we
Or aren't we?
Together?
That of course,
Remains
To be seen.

SPOONING

Spooning

Spooning has dual meaning
Whereas I've read the book by Ed.
It once meant nestled bodies,
While laying close in bed.
It's now a bit more literal,
It does involve a spoon;
Lotion, if desired,
Perhaps a dim-lit room.
A teaspoon or a tablespoon?
Your preference or try twice.
No batteries required for
This handy smooth device.
If Webster's were to redefine
The meaning of the spoon,
The prudes on staff might blush
Or choose to leave the room.
For those of you who've read it,
You know just what I mean.
For those who've not, well then...
That clearly REMAINS TO BE SEEN.

(From a satisfied reader.)

book SAMPLING

Read the opening pages here.
Remains To Be Seen—An Erotic Thriller by
EDWARD H. ESSEX

Edward's erotic novel *Remains To Be Seen* is available for Kindle and as a paperback from Amazon.com. It is also available for Nook from barnesandnoble.com (Nookie for Nook?)

Remains To Be Seen has garnered five star Amazon reader reviews:

I loved Remains To Be Seen. But beyond the passages of erotic romance, I found an even more compelling story about the devastating effect an all-consuming, passionate affair can have upon an intelligent and powerful, yet fragile, person drawn into an emotional whirlpool.

Remains To Be Seen is erotic, sexy and a page turner. I could not put this book down. A must read…for all!

Thoroughly enjoyed this page turner.....cuddled up on the sofa during a snowstorm with a pot of tea and this one....loved the references to colloquial British expressions, and the heat is hot!! Would love to learn how to do that with the back side of a spoon! Totally enraptured me with the passion with which these lovers entice and pleased each other....that the characters are introduced as if in a play and then completely developed within the story was also a pleasant change from the common format that an erotic romance usually takes. Mr. Essex throwing in the thriller ending just was the cherry on top. Hoping to meet Phillip one day in a local shop…

The sequel, *What Remains?* will be released late Summer 2014. Edward will also be releasing *Foreplay*, a collection of naughty bedtime stories *to get you in the mood.*

Remains To Be Seen 2013 © Copyright Words In The Works LLC

ISBN: 978-0-9910364-1-7

Publisher: Words In The Works LLC

info@wordsintheworks.com

The Players

Phillip is an alcoholic and his drinking was largely responsible for the end of his marriage. But he's in recovery and doing well. He's not looking to jump straight into another relationship but the company of a good woman wouldn't go amiss.

Susan is a beautiful English woman of a certain age. She has been married to the same man for many years. Despite living a comfortable life in upscale Chester County, she feels lonely. Her distraction is her antiques shop, *Remains To Be Seen.*

James is Susan's husband. He was raised the son of a British Army officer and followed family tradition by joining the forces. He fought in Northern Ireland during the troubles of the 1970's—an experience that left him with emotional scars.

Sarah is a few years older than Susan. She was Susan's boss back in the soaring seventies in London. When Susan left for America, Sarah followed. Sarah was the object of Susan's brief foray into lesbianism, an experience neither woman got over.

Jennifer is Phillip's bisexual twin sister. She lives with a woman in L.A. where she works in the movie business. Phillip and Jennifer have an unusually—some might say, uncomfortably—close relationship.

Phillip

The parking situation in Old Woodford Village on weekends was awful. It was a tiny village and there simply wasn't anywhere to add more parking spaces as the car population grew over the years. There were only a few businesses. A corner grocery store, a couple of real estate offices, a little restaurant, and a furnishing shop that always appeared to be closed. But the village also boasted the only movie theater in the area. As a result, the only legal places to park—a small blacktopped area behind the theater itself and a few roadside spaces—were always full well before the film started. It wasn't unusual to see a procession of seven or eight cars in front of the theater at showtime as frustrated drivers dropped off their passengers, urging them to go ahead and buy the tickets while they circled the village in search of a parking space they knew didn't exist.

Making matters worse was Officer Todd. Woodford was far enough north of Manhattan to leave the wickedness of the big city behind, and since it was populated for the most part by wealthy commuters and weekenders, it saw very little in the way of crime. This left the local policeman plenty of time to be extra vigilant in the parking offense department. And sure enough, Saturday afternoons would see him marching—was that a smirk on his face?—from one car to another, marking tires with his chalk stick and making sure no one overstayed their welcome.

Having missed not only the upcoming attractions and the commercials for the Chinese restaurant in nearby Kimpton, but the beginning of several movies as well, I became wise to this parking dilemma.

When I wanted to see an afternoon movie, I made sure I arrived at least an hour ahead of time. Armed with the New York Times and the Post, I would then have a coffee and sandwich in the little restaurant next to the theater and catch up on all the news—juicy gossip in the Post's case— before the movie started.

It was on one such Saturday in early November that I met Susan.

I had parked my car behind the theater as usual and was heading towards the restaurant when I saw a freshly painted sign that simply said *Parking*. An arrow pointed to three car spaces in front of what looked like an unused garage. I thought I'd made a discovery—a new parking spot no less—until I saw that the spaces were reserved for *Remains To Be Seen* only.

Looking up above the garage, I saw a small clapboard house. I remembered it being someone's home at one time but now had been converted for the sole purpose of selling *Antique China and Silver from England* as a second elegantly lettered sign over the doorway read.

Thanks to my usual early arrival in the village, there was plenty of time before the movie started.

Being from England myself—although at fifty-one, not yet an antique—I decided to take a quick look inside the shop before having lunch.

Susan

The shop had only been open a week or so when I first met Phillip. I knew immediately that he was English by the way he hesitantly put his head around the door, almost as if this were my home and he needed to ask permission before coming in.

—Good afternoon, he said.

—Good afternoon. Please, come on in.

—Thanks. Is this new? The shop I mean, not the china and silver obviously.

He smiled as he said it. He had a nice smile.

—Yes, I replied. —We opened this week.

—I noticed the parking spaces first.

—They are a bit of a premium in the village, aren't they? I had to provide some otherwise I'd never get any customers.

—Yes, of course. Very clever name for an antiques shop, *Remains To Be Seen*.

—Thank you. Bit of a pun though.

—That's what the English are good at, isn't it? You are from England, aren't you?

—Yes, I am. Been here donkey's years though!

Phillip laughed at the Englishness of the expression as if he hadn't heard it for donkey's years. We introduced ourselves.

—Susan Birley.

—Phillip Brown.

And then we exchanged the usual—How long have you been in the States? What brought you here? Do you miss England? All the questions the English in America always ask each other. The chitchat went on a bit longer and then he glanced around the shop.

—May I look around?

—Of course.

He was very nice. A nice, polite Englishman.

Phillip

I didn't go back to Woodford Village for three or four weeks after that.

I had my children over the Thanksgiving holiday. And then the next couple of weekends were taken up with Christmas shopping.

By the third weekend in December, I was sick of fighting the crowds at the mall and decided to have that Saturday to myself. With the exception of my business partner and his family, I had bought all of my presents. I had spent a fortune on my kids. Kate was fifteen and learning guitar. Her wish list included amplifiers, guitar stands, and carrying cases—music is an expensive hobby. William, at twelve, was still into video games and anything to do with computers. It was the first Christmas after my divorce from their mother and I wondered whether I had been subconsciously compensating by buying them so much. I didn't dwell on it.

I got up late, made coffee, and went out to pick up the newspapers from the end of my driveway. I checked the movie listings as I walked back to the house.

Jane Eyre was playing in Old Woodford. How very English. I decided I would go to the 2:00 showing. It would also give me an excuse to drop into *Remains To Be Seen*. I could chat with Susan about the film.

—Had she seen it? Was she going to see it? Shouldn't she? Being English and all?

I suddenly felt like a schoolboy. Why was I looking for an excuse to see Susan?

She was around fifty-five, fifty-six. She looked married even though she wasn't wearing a wedding ring. She had that self-assurance about her, the security of having had a long relationship with one man. Of having raised a family and now with them all grown up and living away from home, having opened a little business to keep busy.

That was probably what she was all about.

She was also very, very attractive. In that mature, sophisticated woman, kind of way.

I drove to Old Woodford, listening to classical music on the local public broadcasting station. It provided a bland background for the thoughts going around in my mind. I found myself very excited at the prospect of seeing Susan. I obviously couldn't keep going in the shop without buying something. My business partner and his wife were great lovers of Colman's English Mustard—the real stuff, the hot powder you mixed with water—and I had noticed a beautiful silver mustard pot dated 1910 in the shop that would be the perfect gift for them. English mustard in a silver English mustard pot! I would wrap a tin of Colman's as well and give them that first, telling them *that* was their big gift. They liked a laugh. I parked in the theatre lot, gathered up the newspapers that had slid off the passenger seat and all over the floor of the car as I had wound my way around the country lanes on the way to the village, and hurried across the street to the shop.

I felt like I was on a first date. That mixture of excitement, a strange empty feeling in the stomach, and a slight dizziness at the prospect of seeing Susan.

—How are you today? Can I help you?

The question had come not from Susan, but a perfectly pleasant, nicely dressed woman probably just a little older than Susan.

—Oh, I was looking for a present for someone. The last time I was here I spoke to…Susan was it?

For some reason, I pretended not to remember Susan's name.

—Yes, Susan. She went back to London last night for Christmas. The woman smiled a polite smile. —To spend it with her husband's family. And then on to her home near Dublin.

—Oh, I said again. Her husband's family. My heart stupidly started beating faster, as if I had been caught doing something wrong. I tried to think of something to say that would cover up the look of disappointment on my face.

—No doubt hunting for more silver and china while she's there, I said.

—That's right, yes. You said you were looking for a present?

—Yes.

—Well, I can help you if you'd like. I'm Sarah. An old friend of Susan's. She smiled as she said Susan's name. —Well, not old in the sense of being old, I've just known her a long time.

—Yes. Of course.

She laughed at her little joke. I didn't. I just wanted to leave.

The mustard pot was still on display among an eclectic collection of china and bric-a-brac on an oval table in the middle of the shop. I picked it up and paid for it.

Sarah

It was pretty obvious why Phillip had come into the shop. Susan had that effect on men.

I had my share of men too, of course. Timothy was the last. He changed my life. Literally.

Timothy was a lot older than me. I was twenty-five at the time; he was fifty-two. Old enough to be my father as they say. This was before I got into the advertising agency side of marketing. I was working in London for a radio station selling advertising airtime. Timothy had worked in all the agencies for years—he knew everyone in that world. He had got fed up with all the politics and clients who were still wet behind the ears ripping his work apart. So he started his own little consulting business. He ticked over rather nicely with three or four small accounts and a couple of gigs a year working for the big boys in the main agency world. He moved from just copywriting to design work, and then new product development. He was a one-man band in that he also planned media for his clients and handled the day-to-day administration of their businesses. He was working with a client who had a salad dressing recipe—a family heirloom—when I met him. He had found a food producer who could make the recipe on a commercial scale. He named the product and designed the packaging. He wrote all the advertising. This included a campaign of very clever radio commercials. My name had been given to him by one of his ad world contacts and he called me to set up an appointment. He wanted to go over all the usual stuff. Demographics. Reach. Rates.

—I need to get some numbers as soon as possible. Could you come to my office? It's in my home. A bit out of central London though.

—That's okay, I said. —Where are you?

—Islington. On one of the streets behind the Angel pub.

I went quiet.

—I live in Camden Passage.

—Are you serious?

We were five minutes from each other.

—Well, do you want to come over early? Before you go into your office?

—That would be great. Shall I get there around 9:00?

—Yes. I'll have coffee on.

He gave me his address. —I'll see you then, Timothy.

Timothy was gorgeous. W*ell-preserved* is the term people tend to use, isn't it? But he really *didn't* look fifty-two. He was a big man. Not particularly tall, maybe your standard five-ten. Big in that he was stocky. Big barrel of a chest. Little bit of a gut hanging below that robust rib cage. But it all looked perfectly placed. The overall picture from neck down was rather pleasant. And then there was his face. Thin lips that often broke into a wide smile. Eyes that sparkled when he was talking. Hair that was thick and lush, parting naturally down the middle. He invented the word *charm*.

We flirted blatantly with each other. He kissed me on the cheek when I left. I couldn't stop thinking about him. What would it be like? With an older man? The cliché. All that stuff about experience. A lesson in sex. Was it true? When I had the radio numbers together, I called him. We arranged a second visit. Same time, same place. I found myself chatting away merrily to him. He was so easy to be with. A funny man. For some reason, I told him I was slow out of bed that morning— that it had taken me a long time to get ready.

—Well, you look beautiful. If I were 20 years younger...
He flashed a glance and let the thought drift.
I felt that old tingle downstairs.
—Timothy, forget being younger. You're gorgeous right now.

I couldn't believe I had come right out and said it. He laughed. We both did. As I stood up to leave, I reached across the table to gather up my things. I could feel my sweater riding up, exposing a band of skin. I could also feel his eyes on me. I turned towards him and tugged at the bottom of the sweater. Pulled it back down. He smiled. And I knew what that particular smile meant.

By my third visit, I was certain I was going to sleep with him. I got wet simply walking over there. I had put on a skirt this time—I wanted him to see my legs. High-ish heels. Well, okay. High heels. No stockings.

He opened the door with his usual smile. He kissed me on the cheek just as he had done the previous two times I visited.

Something took hold of me. I grabbed his face in my hands. I didn't let him turn away. Our eyes locked on each other. I simply leaned in and kissed him. Once. Then again. Then a little bit longer. Then my arms were around his neck. His went around my waist. We lost our balance but not our contact as he pulled me into the hallway and pushed the front door shut. We fell against the wall. The kissing getting more and more intense. His body was hard up against me. And I mean hard. I could feel his cock through his trousers. I reached down and stroked it lightly. I cupped my hands under his balls. We slid down the wall and rolled onto the carpet runner. It scooted away from us until we were laying at an angle to it. Half on the carpet. Half on the polished wood floor.

—Let's go to the other room, he whispered in my ear.

THE AUTHOR

Before turning to books, Edward H. Essex was an award-winning advertising writer and art director. He began his career in his native England, moved to Los Angeles in 1979, and then settled in New York in 1988. He has won all the important advertising industry awards including London's Design & Art Directors Association, New York One Show Gold, New York Art Directors Club, Effie's for advertising effectiveness, Clio Awards, and Cannes Film Festival Silver and Bronze Lions.

He left the ad industry in 1993 to start a company that helps small businesses get started and to concentrate on writing. He lives in New York and has two grown children.

Made in the USA
San Bernardino, CA
17 July 2014